REENTERING YOUR COMMUNITY

A Handbook

WHAT IS THIS HANDBOOK FOR?

Reentering your community can be more manageable when you're aware of services and resources available to help.

This handbook contains 3 checklists:
- **for before your release,**
- **just after you return home,**
- **and later, when you're a bit more settled in.**

It also includes additional information in specific areas where you may have questions or be looking for tools available to you.

Be sure to review these lists, and discuss them and questions you may have with your Case Manager, Bureau Social Worker, or Reentry Affairs Coordinator.

Reentry can be a complicated process – others have felt the same way. But many of them were able to overcome this and have succeeded in finding work, supporting themselves and their families, and more. We want you to achieve the same.

You are a member of your community, and we want to help you transition home and succeed. If you have any questions, don't hesitate to call the **Bureau of Prisons Reentry Hotline (toll-free)** at **1-877-895-9196**.

2-1-1 is a free and confidential service that helps people find the local resources they need (including reentry services) 24 hours a day, 7 days a week by calling **2-1-1** or by visiting **www.211.org**.

WHAT'S IN THIS GUIDE?

CHECKLIST #1:
THINGS TO DO
BEFORE YOUR RELEASE

TIMELINE: Start this at least 8 weeks before you leave.

☐ **Get your identification documents.**

Talk with your **Case Manager or Reentry Affairs Coordinator** about this, because they can help you.

- You can get a **social security card** or a replacement card for free from the Social Security Administration. If you do not get your card before you leave prison, the application and other information can be found at **https://www.ssa.gov/ssnumber**

- **Birth certificates** can be ordered while you are in prison from the state where you were born. If you do not get your birth certificate before you leave prison, this website shows you where to write for vital records for each state and territory: **http://www.cdc.gov/nchs/w2w.htm**

☐ **Get proof of your GED / high school completion, or any other classes you took while in prison.**

- If you got your GED while in prison, make sure you have your transcript before you are released. *The Bureau does not keep or give GED transcripts post-release.*

- If you can, create a folder with everything positive you have done while in prison, including certificates for vocational training, drug treatment, anger management or any other cognitive behavioral therapy.

☐ **Get your medical records.**

Ask **Health Services** about getting copies of your medical records while you are still in prison to help you transition to treatment in the community.

☐ **Confirm your housing.**

Your **Reentry Affairs Coordinator, Case Manager, or Social Worker** (if available) can provide you information about finding a place to live in your release city. **Social Workers** can also help if you need special housing such as a nursing home, assisted living, senior housing, or group home placement.

☐ **Find out about any outstanding fees, fines, debts, or warrants.**

Speak to your **Case Manager** about how to find out if you have any outstanding fees, fines, warrants or debts. These can limit your ability to obtain employment, housing, or even lead to arrest. If you have outstanding child support payments, failing to manage this before your release could prevent you from getting a driver's license.

☐ **Are you a veteran? If yes, make sure you have your military discharge papers.**

You can do this either online (after your release) or by mail. If you choose to do by mail, check with your **Case Manager** to see if they can give you the paper form. Instructions and forms for both online and by mail can be found at http://www.archives. gov/veterans/military-service-records/

CHECKLIST #2:
THINGS TO DO IMMEDIATELY AFTER YOUR RETURN

TIMELINE: Do these in your first week of reentry.

If you are transitioning through a **Residential Reentry Center**, staff at the center will be able to assist you with some of the items on this checklist.

☐ **Find somewhere to access the internet.**

Most public libraries offer *free* internet access (although photo identification may be required) and library staff can help you. Most **Residential Reentry Centers (RRCs)** also have internet services.

☐ **Create an email address.**

Many websites (for example **www.gmail.com or www.yahoo.com**) allow you to set-up a free email account. To make it simple and professional, use your first name and last name, or some combination of your initials. Write it down:

_____

(ex. johndoe@gmail.com)

☐ **Get a photo ID.**

You can obtain one through your local **Department of Motor Vehicles**. To find your local Department of Motor Vehicles, and know what documents to bring (probably your birth certificate and/or social security card), visit www.usa.gov/motor-vehicle-services

☐ **Sign-up for Health Insurance.**

The Affordable Care Act has created *free* or low-cost health care coverage options and improved access to health care services.

- If you need low-cost health insurance, go to the **Health Insurance Marketplace** (www.healthcare.gov.) The website helps individuals find and sign up for health care coverage and those who qualify can also sign up for **Medicaid**. *Upon release, you have a 60-day special enrollment period to sign up.*

- You can also call **1-800-318-2596 (TTY: 1-855-889-4325) 24/7** if you don't have a computer or need help. *The phone line is closed Memorial Day, July 4th, Labor Day, Thanksgiving Day, and Christmas Day.*

- **Are you a veteran?** If yes, you may qualify for healthcare through the **Department of Veterans Affairs**. Information about your health benefits as a veteran can be found at: http://www.va.gov/healthbenefits/apply/veterans.asp

☐ Are you under age 26?

If yes, confirm your **selective service status**. Your status may be required by employers or for student loans.

- Call toll-free **1-888-655-1825**

- Young men in prison do not have to register while they are committed. However, they **must register within 30 days after being released** if they have not yet reached their 26th birthday.

☐ Get proof of your GED / high school completion

- If you earned your high school diploma before you were in prison, you can get a copy from the **Department of Education** for the state where you attended high school. Contact information can be found at: **www2.ed.gov/about/contacts/state/**. GED certificates can be requested from the state's **GED Administrator** where you took the test: **www.gedtestingservice.com/testers/ged-testing-administrator**.

CHECKLIST #3:
THINGS TO DO TO REBUILD

TIMELINE: Do these in your first month of reentry.

☐ **Take control of your finances.**

To qualify for certain benefits, you will need to understand your current debts, bills, and other payments. Having a bank account and using free tools can help you manage this. See the *"Managing Your Money"* section on page 11.

☐ **Connect with assistance programs and community organizations that can help.**

Once you understand your finances, apply for benefit programs that can help you get food and other necessities. Community organizations are also ready to help. See the *"Getting Support"* section on page 15.

☐ **Don't forget to take care of yourself!**

You have a lot going on, but making sure to stay healthy and keeping on track with any medications or appointments will help you complete all the other things you need to do. See the *"Taking Care of Your Physical and Mental Health"* section on page 21.

☐ **Continue your education.**

There are many ways to build your skills and qualify for better jobs. See the *"Building Your Skills"* section on page 25.

☐ **Begin your job search.**

See the *"Finding a Job"* section on page 27.

☐ **If you need legal assistance, connect with organizations that do this for free.**

Many non-profits exist to support you if you experience discrimination or other injustice. To better understand your rights, reach out to one of these organizations. See the *"Seeking Legal Assistance"* section on page 31.

☐ **Focus on re-building your relationships.**

Reconnecting with loved ones and having them support your transition can be incredibly empowering. However, it will take time and patience. See the *"Rebuilding Relationships"* section on page 35.

MANAGING YOUR MONEY

Setting Up a Bank Account

Having a bank account with a debit card will really help to organize your finances. To learn more about how to select a checking account that is right for you, check out the **Consumer Financial Protection Bureau's (CFPB)** resource on this: http://www.consumerfinance.gov/blog/guides-to-help-you-open-and-manage-your-checking-account/

Most banks will require the following information to open an account:

- **Identification**: A valid, government-issued photo ID.

- **Personal information details**: Name, date of birth, address, phone number, and Social Security number.

- **Money**: Cash, a check, a money order, or funds you can electronically transfer into the new account.

Understanding Your Credit

You are entitled to a *free* copy of your **credit report**, once a year. Your credit report may be used for background screening for employment and housing. To order your free report:

- Online – www.annualcreditreport.com
- Phone – **1-877-322-8228**

Asking General Questions

CFPB also has a frequently-asked questions section, where people can learn important financial information. Questions like the following are answered at:
http://www.consumerfinance.gov/askcfpb/

- *My employer says I have to have direct deposit. Everywhere I go, the banks and credit unions seem to charge fees. How can I find the right account for me?*

- *My credit report has information that's not accurate. How can I fix it?*

- *Should I borrow money from my credit card or take out a small loan to cover my bills until my next paycheck?*

Another government website that provides tools and guidance to managing your money is:
www.MyMoney.gov

Filing Taxes and Getting Credits

If you do obtain a job, you may be eligible for a refundable tax credit (the Earned-Income Tax Credit – EITC) that encourages work and makes up for other taxes, such as payroll taxes. Millions of working families and individuals qualify for EITC; however, you must file a tax return.

- For *free* tax preparation assistance: http://irs.treasury.gov/freetaxprep/

- To estimate the value of your EITC credit: http://www.cbpp.org/research/federal-tax/policy-basics-the-earned-income-tax-credit

Managing Payments

Child Support: As mentioned in Checklist #1, managing your child support requirements is incredibly important. If you have a child support order, you may be able to apply for a modification from the court to have your child support order reduced to reflect a lack of earnings or low earnings. You may also be eligible to participate in programs that may help you find a job, reinstate your driver's license, offer parenting education, or help reduce the amount of child support debt you owe. Legal Aid offices may be able to help with legal representation in child support cases.

- The contact information for Child Support offices in each state, and some tribes, can be found at: http://www.acf.hhs.gov/programs/css/resource/state-and-tribal-child-support-agency-contacts

- A state-by-state guide for how to apply for a modification of a child support order can be found at: http://www.acf.hhs.gov/programs/css/state-by-state-how-to-change-a-child-support-order

- This guide on Changing a Child Support Order has more information: www.acf.hhs.gov/sites/default/files/programs/css/changing_a_child_support_order.pdf

Student Loan Debt

Having a student loan in default also prevents the release of a new student loan, harming your ability to continue your education. If you're not sure about your student loans, verify your loan status.

1. **Call the Department of Education** at **(800) 621-3115** or check the National Student Loan Data System website (www.nslds.ed.gov) to make sure there is no loan for you on file.

2. **If you have a loan in default**, there are several options available to you, including Income-Driven Repayment plans, to help you manage this. You can learn more and connect with someone that can help you think about this at: https://studentaid.ed.gov/sa/repay-loans

GETTING SUPPORT

Navigating Assistance Programs

Programs that are available are outlined in this section. However, navigating these one at a time can be complicated. Reach out to Community Organizations that can help you identify and apply for programs that are right for you.

- **United Way**: United Way agencies are non-profit organizations offering services to individuals and families in need. Many United Way agencies give housing assistance or referrals to supportive housing, nursing homes, and other residential programs in your area. In most communities, United Way agencies can be reached by dialing **2-1-1** or by going to: **www.unitedway.org/find-your-united-way/**

- **Salvation Army**: The Salvation Army has a network of shelters and programs across the nation. When available, they may be able to give lodging, clothing, food, and a cash grant for the first 90 days after you are released from RRC placement. You can find more information about the Salvation Army on their website at: **www.salvationarmy.org**

- **Goodwill Industries International, Inc.**: Goodwill helps individuals and families with education, skills training, and job placement services, as well as helps with supporting services such as transportation, housing, and clothing. You can find out about Goodwill services in your area by going to: www.goodwill.org

Are you a veteran?

A variety of benefits are available to individuals who have served in the United States military. For more information go to: www.benefits.va.gov/benefits/ and for housing support, call **1-877-424-3838**.

Income Assistance Programs

- **Temporary Assistance for Needy Families (TANF)**: The Department of Health and Human Services gives employment services and cash assistance to low-income families. To learn eligibility criteria and how to apply in your state, go to: http://www.acf.hhs.gov/programs/ofa/help

- **Supplemental Security Income (SSI)**: Provides money to low-income individuals who are either age 65 or older, blind, or disabled. For more information go to: www.ssa.gov/disabilityssi/ssi.html

- **Social Security Disability Insurance (SSDI)**: Provides income to people with physical or mental problems that are severe enough to prevent them from working. Information can be found at: www.ssa.gov/disabilityssi/

- **Unemployment Insurance (UI)**: Unemployment Insurance provides temporary financial help to workers who are unemployed through no fault of their own. Eligibility, as well as the amount and length of benefits, are determined by each state. Usually, you will have to have been employed for some time before you can collect UI. More information can be found at: http://www.careeronestop.org/ReEmployment/UnemploymentBenefits/am-i-eligible.aspx

Food Assistance Programs

- **Supplemental Nutrition Assistance Program (SNAP)**: The Department of Agriculture gives nutrition assistance to eligible low-income individuals and families. In order to receive benefits, families must meet certain financial and non-financial criteria. (Note: If you are receiving Temporary Assistance for Needy Families (TANF), you are automatically eligible.) To learn eligibility criteria and how to apply in your state, go to: http://www.fns.usda.gov/snap/apply

Note: A federal law prohibits anyone convicted of a drug felony from receiving SNAP or TANF; however, most states have limited or eliminated that ban. For more information on your eligibility, see: www.pewtrusts.org/en/research-and-analysis/blogs/stateline/2015/07/30/states-rethink-restrictions-on-food-stamps-welfare-for-drug-felons

- **Emergency Food Assistance Program (TEFAP)**: Each state sets requirements to determine who is eligible to receive free food. More information, including how to apply, is found at: **www.fns.usda.gov/tefap/ eligibility-and-how-apply**

- **Commodity Supplemental Food Program (CSFP)**: The U.S. Department of Agriculture also purchases food and makes it available to CSFP agencies in each state for low-income people at least 60 years of age. More information can be found at: **www.fns.usda.gov/csfp/ eligibility-how-apply**

Housing Assistance

The U.S. Department of Housing and Urban Development (HUD) provides low-cost housing assistance to those who qualify. These programs generally are managed by local government agencies.

- You can get help finding local housing and shelters by calling 1-800-569-4287 or going to: **http://resources.hud.gov/** and clicking on "Find Homeless Services Near Me."

- If you are not able to secure housing through a program or through family or friends, you may wish to contact a "Continuum of Care" who may be able to provide you with short- or long-term assistance. To find a Continuum of

Care (CoC) in your area, go to: https://www.hudexchange.info/programs/coc/ and click on "Contact a CoC" to search.

Note: Some local housing authorities restrict access to housing for those with a criminal conviction, but many will consider any rehabilitative programming you have received (such as RDAP) and your family support system in their decision.

Transportation Assistance

Getting to medical appointments, job interviews, or other important meetings can be difficult if you don't have a car. Public transportation is usually the most inexpensive option, and each city and state has their own programs to help with the cost of public transportation. Your local community organization can help you navigate this. Additionally, here are some other options:

- **Rural Transit Assistance Programs**: These help the millions of Americans that live in cities of less than 50,000 people. To contact and learn more about transportation support in your state, go to: http://nationalrtap.org/findanything/Appendices/State-RTAP-5311-Websites and click on the RTAP and/or 5311 site for your state.

- **Public Transportation and Mass Transit**: Check your city for bus, subway, light railway, or regional railway express options. Public transit schedules are always available for free online. Special assistance such as reduced fares or services for the elderly and disabled exist as well, but you'll need to check locally for details.

- **Walking/Bicycling**: If you can, plan to live within walking or bicycling distance to work, shopping, and your family. To learn more about biking laws, safety tips, and other best practices about biking, check out: http://bikeleague.org/ridesmart

- **Ridesharing/Carpools**: Carpools can save you money in commuting expenses. Some carpools pick up riders at their homes, meet at a place everyone agrees on, or in a commuter lot. If you want to learn more about options available in your state, a quick search online will help you find sites like: http://www.rideshare-directory.com/ that have different message boards and ways to connect with others interested.

- **Taxi Cabs**: Typically, cabs are a convenient form of transportation; however, they can also be the most expensive. If you have a smartphone and services are available in your area, transportation applications (for example: "LyftLine," "UberX," and "UberPool") offer lower-cost options. You can learn more about these services, and the costs, on their websites.

TAKING CARE OF YOUR PHYSICAL AND MENTAL HEALTH

Maintaining Your Physical Health

Once you have health insurance, you will be able to go to any health care provider who accepts your health insurance plan. Finding a **primary care provider** is the best way to manage your health instead of going to the Emergency Room or Urgent Care – it will save you money and time and increase the likelihood of staying healthy.

You may be referred to specialty doctors for specific health concerns. Visit these providers as soon as possible. You should also get your vision checked at least once a year, and your teeth cleaned once every six months to help prevent more serious problems in the future.

If you need **health care right away**, you can find a community clinic here: http://www.findahealthcenter.hrsa.gov.

Are you a veteran?

You can find your nearest VA medical center here: http://www.va.gov/directory/guide/division_flsh.asp?dnum=1

Using Mental Health Services

Adjusting to life outside of prison can be difficult at times; you may find yourself feeling discouraged or depressed. Many people – millions of Americans, in fact – experience some kind of mental health challenge, whether it is depression, anxiety, or some form of addiction. You should feel comfortable asking any questions you have about your mental health with your primary care provider – and know that checkups and services for these are covered by most insurance companies as any other health service.

- Additionally, you can find free or low-cost mental health services available in your area on the **Substance Abuse and Mental Health Services Administration (SAMHSA)** website: **https:// findtreatment.samhsa.gov/** or by calling the **National Helpline 1-800-662-HELP/4357 (TDD: 1-800-487-4889**).

- No matter what problems you are dealing with, there is a reason to keep on living. By calling **1-800-273-TALK (8255)** at any time, you will be connected to a counselor at a crisis center in your area. You can also visit the **National Suicide Prevention Lifeline** website at: **www.suicidepreventionlifeline.org**.

Keeping Up with Drug Treatment Services

Many people who are returning to the community have a history of abusing substances like alcohol and illegal or prescription drugs. You may have participated in treatment while incarcerated, and it is important to maintain a drug-free lifestyle after release.

Ask your **Drug Abuse Program Coordinator** or **Community Treatment Services Provider** if he or she can help you find a treatment or support program before your release. If you have a supervised release plan, your **Probation Officer** may be able to arrange for you to participate in a substance abuse treatment program.

- Most communities have self-help support groups. Local **Alcoholics Anonymous** and **Narcotics Anonymous** meetings can be found here:

  - **www.aa.org/pages/en_US/find-local-aa**

  - **www.na.org/meetingsearch/**

- You can find a drug treatment facility by visiting the **Substance Abuse and Mental Health Services Administration (SAMHSA)** website at https://findtreatment.samhsa.gov/ or by calling the National Helpline **(1-800-662-HELP/4357; 1-800-487-4889 TDD)**

- The following organizations may be able to help you find other support and treatment resources in your local area:

  - National Drug Information Treatment and Referral Hotline: **1-(800)-662-HELP**

  - National Mental Health Association: **(703) 684-7722 voice, (800) 969-6642 info line**

  - National Health Information Center: **(800) 336-4797**

- National Clearinghouse for Alcohol and Drug Information (NCADI): **1-(800)-729-6686**

- National Mental Health Knowledge Exchange Network (KEN): **1-(800)-789-2647**

- American Council on Alcoholism: **(703) 248-9005**

Forgot to get your medical records before your release?

You'll need to send a letter to the **Federal Bureau of Prisons.**

The letter must specifically describe the records you want and provide the following: full name, register number, birthdate, where you were born, and the address where you want your records to be mailed. To protect your privacy, the letter must either be **notarized** (you will need to have a notary public sign the letter) or you must include a signed **Form DOJ-361, Certification of Identity**. The form can be found at: http://www.bop.gov/foia/DOJ361.pdf. Notaries are commonly found at banks, city halls and county courthouses.

Mail this letter to:

FOIA/PA Section
Office of General Counsel, Room 924
Federal Bureau of Prisons
320 First Street, N.W.
Washington, DC 20534

BUILDING YOUR SKILLS

Having an education is important because it increases employment options. There are many ways to further your education upon release.

Adult Basic Education (ABE) programs are for individuals who want to improve in reading, writing, math, listening, and speaking. ABE programs are offered at adult schools, career centers, libraries, or community colleges for *free* or for a small fee.

If you do not have a high school diploma or GED, you should enroll in a GED program as soon as possible after release. The GED test allows adults who have not completed high school to show they have the knowledge and skills associated with a high school diploma. Many community colleges offer programs that allow you to earn a GED and college credits at the same time.

- You can find GED test preparation classes near you at: **www.gedtestingservice.com/testers/ locate-a-prep-center** or by calling the *toll-free* number **1-800-MY-GED (1-800-626-9433)**.

If you have a high school diploma or GED and want to further your education, there are resources available to help you with the cost of college. Community colleges are a common option for individuals returning home from prison. The low cost of tuition and the variety of programs offered make these colleges an ideal starting place. By enrolling in a community college, you can earn an Associate's degree and then transfer to a four-year college or university to earn a Bachelor's degree.

- The **Free Application for Federal Student Aid (FAFSA)** is the starting point for accessing all federal student financial aid. You can find FAFSA online at: http://www.fafsa.gov or you can request a paper copy from **1-800-4-FED-AID (1-800-433-3243).**

- Federal student aid information can be found at: http://www.StudentLoans.gov

Vocational programs provide you with skills required for a particular job. They are also referred to as occupational, votech, or career and technical education programs. Vocational programs are available through community and technical colleges, as well as trade schools, and they take less time to complete than academic college degree programs.

- You can apply at the local employment office, as a "displaced worker," for **Department of Labor Second Chance Act** funds if you want to learn a vocational trade.

Are you a veteran?

You may qualify for education benefits: http://www.benefits.va.gov/gibill/index.asp

FINDING A JOB

Being prepared will improve your chances of finding a job.

1. **Make sure your background information is accurate.** Many companies do screenings that may include criminal record information.

   - In the "Employment Screening" section of the following link, you can find reporting agencies that will give you a *free* report every 12 months: **http://files.consumerfinance. gov/f/201501_cfpb_list-consumer-reporting-agencies.pdf**

2. **Outline steps for your job hunt** by visiting the Department of Labor's "Career One Stop" at: **www.careeronestop.org**

   - On this site, you can do everything from find trainings, resume guides, interview tips, to search job databases.

3. **Create an "application package"** by putting together a draft resume and collect the items you put together during Checklist #1 (certificates, activities you completed in prison, and letters of recommendation.)

4. **Get some feedback on your resume and application package** from someone who is trained to help individuals search, prepare for, and apply to jobs.

- **Call 2-1-1, or connect with other Community Organizations** listed in the "Getting Support" section and ask about employment services.

- **Search for a local American Job Center**: http://www.careeronestop.org/localhelp/americanjobcenters/find-american-job-centers.aspx to meet with an employment counselor.

- **Look up your state's resources through the National HIRE Network**. They have organizations in your state that help people with criminal records find employment: www.hirenetwork.org/

5. **Search for jobs online** at: www.careeronestop.org/JobSearch/findjobs/find-jobs.aspx, but also connect with your local job center or employment assistance organization to learn more about tools that they have to find jobs.

  - Many sites online list companies that have programs in which they hire individuals with conviction histories.

  - **The National Employment Law Project (NELP)** lists the states that have "Banned the Box" or enacted Fair Hiring laws or policies. Go to: www.nelp.org/publication/ban-the-box-fair-chance-hiring-state-and-local-guide/ for more information.

6. Prepare for your interview by following tips at http://www.careeronestop.org/JobSearch/Interview/interview-and-negotiate.aspx.

Some of the basics include:

- **Have a list of your strengths and be ready to talk about them.** What are you good at? What type of work do you enjoy? What experience or skills can you offer an employer?

- **Think** about how you will answer questions about your record.

- **Look** at common interview questions: www.careeronestop.org/JobSearch/Interview/common-interview-questions.aspx.

- **Make sure you are clean and well-dressed.** A local community organization can help you with this.

- **Be on time.** Several days before, plan how you will travel to your interview and what time you will need to leave in order to arrive a few minutes early.

Do not be discouraged if it takes a while to get a job. If potential employers express concern about hiring people with a criminal record, you can tell potential employers about two programs that offer insurance to employers who hire someone with a record:

- **Federal Bonding Program** – Any organization (public or private, nonprofit or profit) providing job placement services to ex-offenders can purchase a bond package to protect the employer against employee theft when they hire at-risk job applicants. Call **1-800-233-2258** or go to **www.bonds4jobs.com**

- **Federal Prison Industries (UNICOR).** If you worked for UNICOR, potential employers should contact UNICOR for information regarding the **Federal Bonding Program** by calling **(202) 305-3800**. The program protects employers against theft. More information can be found at: **www.unicor.gov**

Are you a veteran?

The following resources are available:

- **http://www.va.gov/homeless/employment programs.asp**

- **http://www.dol.gov/vets/**

SEEKING LEGAL ASSISTANCE

You may qualify for *free* legal help (called "legal aid") for civil legal problems that affect your daily life. Getting help in these areas can help you get back on your feet more quickly.

How can legal aid help?

Legal aid providers – lawyers, staff and volunteers – provide *free* legal help in many ways. Legal aid providers can help you figure out your legal need, and can give you advice on your legal options. They can also prepare a court or benefit form for you, and represent you in court.

Do you have a "civil legal problem"?

Here are some examples of the most common civil legal problems that many people face as they leave prison and that legal aid can help you with:

- Getting state-issued **photo identification, birth certificate, social security card**, etc.

- Getting a **driver's license**

- **State and federal benefits**, including benefits related to food (SNAP), cash (TANF), and disability (SSI)

- Getting **veteran's benefits**

- **Immigration issues**

- **Housing issues**, including affordable housing, safe housing and avoiding eviction

- **Health care access**, including Medicaid, Medicare, and the Affordable Care Act

- **Safety issues**, including domestic violence, harassment, child abuse and neglect

- **Family issues**, including custody, child support, guardianship and divorce

- **Expunging or sealing your criminal record**

- Getting an **employment or occupational license**

- Dealing with **unpaid tickets, court fines or fees and outstanding warrants**

- **Debt collection** issues

- **Criminal record-based employment discrimination**

Under laws enforced by federal and/or state agencies employers must not treat anyone, including people with criminal records, differently based on their race, national origin, or another reason protected by law.

- **For a simple overview of your rights** as you are applying to jobs, and to better understand what companies are allowed to ask for, read NELP's guide: http://www.nelp.org/content/uploads/2015/03/Guide-for-Workers-Conviction-Arrest-Histories-Know-Your-Rights.pdf

- If you believe you may have experienced **illegal discrimination**, you can file a charge with the EEOC: http://www.eeoc.gov/employees/howtofile.cfm

Who should I contact?

The following websites will help you find **legal aid providers** by the city, county, zip code and/or legal issue.

- http://www.lawhelp.org/find-help
- www.lsc.gov/what-legal-aid/find-legal-aid
- www.hirenetwork.org/clearinghouse

The American Bar Association (ABA) has a list of legal aid providers who work on reentry issues.

More information can be found at: www.americanbar.org/content/dam/aba/administrative/probono_public_service/lsc_reentry_projects.authcheckdam.pdf

The **Native American Rights Fund (NARF)** has a list of legal organizations that focus on Indian law or serve Native American communities.

Go to: www.narf.org/nill/resources/lawyer.html for more information.

What else should I be thinking about?

Find out if you have the **right to vote** in your state, and if there is anything you need to do to restore your right to vote: **www.nonprofitvote. org/voting-as-an-ex-offender/**

- If you are able to do so, register to vote: **https://vote.usa.gov**

Anyone convicted of a felony is prohibited from **possessing firearms or ammunition**. In addition to physically holding or having a firearm or ammunition on you, "possession" also includes a firearm or ammunition that you have knowledge of, and control over, in an automobile or a home. Possession of a firearm or ammunition can result in new federal charges.

- Some states have also enacted additional restrictions on weapons such as tasers, stun guns, and crossbows. You should check with your **probation officer** or **local law enforcement agency** before you come into possession of any type of weapon.

Are you a veteran?

The **Veterans Administration** has a list of **legal organizations and providers** that work with veterans and active duty service members: **http://www.va.gov/directory/guide/division _flsh.asp?dnum=1**

REBUILDING
YOUR RELATIONSHIPS

For most people reentering their community, it will take some time to get used to life back at home. You may not feel comfortable right away. You and your family and friends will have to make some changes.

Your family members will have attempted to adapt to everyday routines without you there, and may have learned to do things around the house (budgeting, grocery shopping, car repair, and other household chores) that you used to do. It is important to talk to your family about how you are feeling and decide how to take care of these things now that you are home.

Here are some other suggestions that can help:

- **Begin by appreciating the small things** others take for granted – such as privacy, being able to come and go as you please, planning your meals, and more.

- **Avoid talking about life in prison** as your only conversation topic. Practice making "small talk" about daily events instead.

- It will be difficult to catch up on everything that happened while you were away. **Be patient with yourself, and your family and friends.**

- **Understand that things will take time**, for both you and those around you, and that even small steps are important.

Trust takes time to rebuild. As your family learns to trust you, they will do so more and more and you will begin to feel more comfortable within your family again. Since you were in prison, a divorce or child custody proceeding may have happened and changed your family as you once knew it.

- **Show your loved ones** that you understand you may have hurt them, and allow them to share painful memories with you.

- **Children** may have become used to living without their mom or dad. They may not understand everything that has happened, where you were, or why you were away. You can ask them if they have any questions, and be patient with them as they readjust.

- **Your parents and your children** are not the same as when you left - do not try to treat them the way you did. They have aged and changed. Show them you care about their needs, are interested in what they are doing, and you want to spend time with them.

- **If you are asked about your incarceration**, answer questions honestly. You do not need to tell them it was "no big deal" or act "tough." Let them know being in prison is no way to spend your life.

Helpful resources about rebuilding relationships with family are available from the National Resource Center for Children and Families of the Incarcerated: **https://nrccfi.camden.rutgers. edu/**. The Resource Center also has a directory of programs specifically designed to help children who have had a parent in prison or jail.

KNOW WHO
TO CONTACT

If you have general questions or need help getting your personal records:

- **Bureau of Prisons Hotline**
  Call **1-877-895-9196** or visit http://www.bop.gov/resources/former_inmate_resources.jsp

If you need free and confidential help obtaining food, housing, health care, employment, counseling and other critical services 24/7 in your area:

- **2-1-1**
  Call **2-1-1** (from either a cell phone or a land line) or visit www.211.org

If you are experiencing a crisis or want to talk to someone for support:

- **Suicide Prevention Lifeline**
  Call **1-800-273-8255**

If you want to find a place to get help navigating services, using a computer, or learn more about services available to you in your community:

- **National Reentry Resource Center (RRC)**
  For more information visit:
  https://csgjusticecenter.org/reentry/reentry-services-directory/

If you are unsure about federal policies that affect people who have been incarcerated, such as not being eligible for certain benefits, not being allowed to live in certain places, or you think you've experienced other discrimination:

- **Reentry Myth Busters**
  Visit **www.csgjusticecenter.org/nrrc/ projects/mythbusters/**

NOTES

www.ingramcontent.com/pod-product-compliance
Lightning Source LLC
Chambersburg PA
CBHW062027280526
45787CB00005B/2240